This Planner Belongs to

Minister Michelle J. Turner
02 - 07 - 06
5 Deer Path Ct, Cary 60013

THE

DREAM

PLANNER

BASED ON
The Dream Giver
BY BRUCE WILKINSON
WITH DAVID & HEATHER KOPP

AUTHOR OF THE #1 *NEW YORK TIMES*
BESTSELLER *The Prayer of Jabez*

Multnomah® Publishers *Sisters, Oregon*

THE DREAM PLANNER

published by Multnomah Publishers, Inc.

© 2003 by Ovation Foundation, Inc.

International Standard Book Number: 1-59052-328-8

Interior images by Steve Gardner, His Image PixelWorks

Scripture quotations are from:

The Holy Bible, New International Version © 1973, 1984 by International Bible Society,
used by permission of Zondervan Publishing House.

Multnomah is a trademark of Multnomah Publishers, Inc.,
and is registered in the U.S. Patent and Trademark Office.
The colophon is a trademark of Multnomah Publishers, Inc.

Printed in the United States of America

For information:

MULTNOMAH PUBLISHERS, INC.

POST OFFICE BOX 1720

SISTERS, OREGON 97759

03 04 05 06 07 08—10 9 8 7 6 5 4 3 2 1 0

"See, the Lord your God has given you the land.

Go up and take possession of it as the Lord,

the God of your fathers, told you.

Do not be afraid; do not be discouraged."

DEUTERONOMY 1:21

Delight yourself in the Lord
and he will give you the desires of your heart.

PSALM 37:4

*Do you not feel yourself drawn by
the expectation and desire of some Great Thing?*

THOMAS TRAHERNE

"In your unfailing love you will lead the people
you have redeemed. In your strength you will guide them
to your holy dwelling"

EXODUS 15:13

*May your heart sing as you
embrace what you were created to be and do.*

THE DREAM GIVER

*Don't get so busy making a living
that you forget what you're living for.*

ANONYMOUS

*Though you have not seen him, you love him;
and even though you do not see him now, you believe in him
and are filled with an inexpressible and glorious joy.*

1 PETER 1:8

The call of God is like the call of the sea;
no one hears it but the one who has the nature of the sea in him.

OSWALD CHAMBERS

*Hitting the scary edge of your Comfort Zone again and again
proves that you're a Dreamer on the move toward your Dream.*

THE DREAM GIVER

May the God of peace, who through the blood
of the eternal covenant brought back from the dead
our Lord Jesus, that great Shepherd of the sheep,
equip you with everything good for doing his will.

HEBREWS 13:20–21

On the other side of that single step—the exact one
Ordinary didn't think he could take—he found that he
had broken through his Comfort Zone. Now the Wall of Fear
was behind him. He was free, and his Dream was ahead.

THE DREAM GIVER

Great All in All, that art my rest, my home;
My way is tedious, and my steps are slow:
Reach forth Thy helpful hand, or bid me come.

FRANCIS QUARLES

"How gladly would I treat you like sons
and give you a desirable land,
the most beautiful inheritance of any nation."

JEREMIAH 3:19

Let the morning bring me word of your unfailing love,
for I have put my trust in you.
Show me the way I should go,
for to you I lift up my soul.

PSALM 143:8

And my God will meet all your needs
according to his glorious riches in Christ Jesus.

PHILIPPIANS 4:19

For you, O Lord, have delivered my soul from death,
my eyes from tears,
my feet from stumbling,
that I may walk before the Lord
in the land of the living.

PSALM 116:8–9

Let us throw off everything that hinders

and the sin that so easily entangles, and let us run

with perseverance the race marked out for us.

Let us fix our eyes on Jesus...who for the joy

set before him endured the cross, scorning its shame....

Consider him who endured such opposition from sinful men,

so that you will not grow weary and lose heart.

HEBREWS 12:1–3

Every noble work is at first impossible.

THOMAS CARLYLE

Leave Him to be the source of all your dreams and joys and delights, and go out and obey what He has said.

OSWALD CHAMBERS

The WasteLand is the place where God
transforms you into the person who can do your Dream.
It is the Dream Giver's loving gift to Dreamers with a future!
THE DREAM GIVER

"*Stand at the crossroads and look;*
ask for the ancient paths,
ask where the good way is, and walk in it,
and you will find rest for your souls."

JEREMIAH 6:16

Severe trouble in a true believer
has the effect of loosening the roots of his soul earthward
and tightening the anchor-hold of his heart heavenward.

CHARLES SPURGEON

Everything you now lack for the upcoming fulfillment
of your Dream is being offered to you in the WasteLand.
God's promise is that you will lack nothing
when you emerge from the other side.

THE DREAM GIVER

*If any of you lacks wisdom, he should ask God,
who gives generously to all without finding fault,
and it will be given to him.*

JAMES 1:5

When the soul gives up all for love,
so that it can have him that is all,
then it finds true rest.

JULIAN OF NORWICH

*Faith is being sure of what we hope for
and certain of what we do not see.*

Hebrews 11:1

The Dream Giver gave my Dream back to me.
Now it is part of his Big Dream—and that means
my Dream is a lot bigger than before.

THE DREAM GIVER

Love finds nothing hard; no task is difficult to the eager.

SAINT JEROME

Each stage or obstacle along our journey
is intended not to block our dream, but to help us
break through to the fulfillment God promises.

THE DREAM GIVER

Then I heard the voice of the Lord saying,
"Whom shall I send? And who will go for us?"
And I said, "Here am I. Send me!"

ISAIAH 6:8

Ordinary knelt by the riverbank and wept with joy.
The Dream Giver was more kind, more good, more wonderful
and trustworthy than he had ever imagined.

For we are God's workmanship, created in Christ Jesus to do good works, which God prepared in advance for us to do.

EPHESIANS 2:10

May I run the race before me,
Strong and brave to face the foe,
Looking only unto Jesus
As I onward go.

KATE B. WILKINSON

*I press on toward the goal to win the prize for which
God has called me heavenward in Christ Jesus.*

PHILIPPIANS 3:14

*Let us consider how we may spur one another on
toward love and good deeds.*

From strength to strength go on, wrestle and fight and pray;
Tread all the powers of darkness down and win the well-fought day.

CHARLES WESLEY

Every step toward Christ kills a doubt.
Every thought, word, and deed for him
carries you away from discouragement.

THEODORE LEDYARD CUYLER

Christ has need of you, dear brothers.
Christ has need of you, dear sisters.

When Ordinary looked at his surrendered Dream,
he saw that it had grown. Now his Dream was no longer
only about Ordinary. Now it was part of the Dream Giver's
Big Dream for the whole world.

THE DREAM GIVER

The way of the Dreamer is difficult—
but anything less is hardly living at all!

THE DREAM GIVER

"For I know the plans I have for you,"

declares the Lord, "plans to prosper you and not to harm

you, plans to give you hope and a future."

JEREMIAH 29:11